Italian - Catalan

Teach Your Child to Read

700 Short Easy Sentences

Name

I Can...

- [ ] read the 1st sentence.
- [ ] read the 2nd sentence.
- [ ] read the 3rd sentence.
- [ ] make my own sentence.
- [ ] color a picture.

La rana sta andando a una festa.

La granota va a una festa.

The frog is going to a party.

La rana verde indossa un cappello verde.

La granota verda porta un barret verd.

The green frog is wearing a green hat.

Name

I Can...

- [ ] read the 1st sentence.
- [ ] read the 2nd sentence.
- [ ] read the 3rd sentence.
- [ ] make my own sentence.
- [ ] color a picture.

A Gufo piace leggere grandi libri.

Owl li agrada llegir grans llibres.

Owl likes to read big books.

Il giovane gufo marrone sta imparando a leggere.

El jove mussol marró està aprenent a llegir.

The young brown owl is learning to read.

Name

I Can...

- ☐ read the 1st sentence.
- ☐ read the 2nd sentence.
- ☐ read the 3rd sentence.
- ☐ make my own sentence.
- ☐ color a picture.

Dai! Il camion dei gelati è qui!

Vinga! Ja està aquí el gelat

Come on! The ice cream truck is here!

Il camion dei gelati sta suonando una bellissima canzone.

El camió de gelats toca una bella cançó.

The ice cream truck is playing a beautiful song.

Name 

I Can...

- ☐ read the 1st sentence.
- ☐ read the 2nd sentence.
- ☐ read the 3rd sentence.
- ☐ make my own sentence.
- ☐ color a picture.

I draghi sono molto amichevoli e hanno delle scale sulla schiena.

Els dracs són molt simpàtics i tenen escales a l'esquena.

Dragons are very friendly and have scales on their backs.

Il grande drago antico ti saluta.

El gran drac antic et saluda.

The big ancient dragon says hello to you.

Name 

I Can...

- [ ] read the 1st sentence.
- [ ] read the 2nd sentence.
- [ ] read the 3rd sentence.
- [ ] make my own sentence.
- [ ] color a picture.

Questo ariete vive nella fattoria.

Aquest moltó viu a la masia.

This ram lives in the farmhouse.

Il montone sorride perché ha appena fatto il bagno.

El moltó somriu perquè només es va banyar.

The ram is smiling because it just took a bath.

Name

I Can...

- [ ] read the 1st sentence.
- [ ] read the 2nd sentence.
- [ ] read the 3rd sentence.
- [ ] make my own sentence.
- [ ] color a picture.

Al coniglietto piace mangiare le carote.

Al conill li agrada menjar pastanagues.

The bunny likes to eat carrots.

Il coniglietto sta portando una carota gigante alla sua famiglia per cena.

El conill porta una pastanaga gegant a la seva família per sopar.

The bunny is bringing a giant carrot to its family for dinner.

Name _______________ 

I Can...

- [ ] read the 1st sentence.
- [ ] read the 2nd sentence.
- [ ] read the 3rd sentence.
- [ ] make my own sentence.
- [ ] color a picture.

Al pagliaccio piace distribuire palloncini ai più piccoli.

Al pallasso li agrada regalar globus als nens.

The clown likes to give out balloons to little kids.

Il pagliaccio tiene in mano tre palloncini colorati.

El pallasso té tres globus de colors.

The clown is holding three colorful balloons.

Name _______________________

I Can...

- [ ] read the 1st sentence.
- [ ] read the 2nd sentence.
- [ ] read the 3rd sentence.
- [ ] make my own sentence.
- [ ] color a picture.

Il pagliaccio si destreggia tra le palle per la sua esibizione.

El pallasso fa maletes per a la seva actuació.

The clown is juggling balls for his performance.

Il buffo clown si destreggia con abilità.

El divertit pallasso fa malabars amb habilitat.

The funny clown is juggling with skill.

Name

I Can...

- [ ] read the 1st sentence.
- [ ] read the 2nd sentence.
- [ ] read the 3rd sentence.
- [ ] make my own sentence.
- [ ] color a picture.

Il coniglietto pasquale distribuirà le uova di cioccolato.

El conill de Pasqua donarà ous de xocolata.

The Easter Bunny is going to give out chocolate eggs.

Il coniglio ha appena strappato alcune carote dal giardino.

El conill acaba de treure algunes pastanagues del jardí.

The rabbit just plucked some carrots out of the garden.

Name _______________ 

I Can...

- [ ] read the 1st sentence.
- [ ] read the 2nd sentence.
- [ ] read the 3rd sentence.
- [ ] make my own sentence.
- [ ] color a picture.

La matita disegna una linea a zig-zag.

El llapis està dibuixant una línia en zig-zag.

The pencil is drawing a zig-zag line.

La matita sta scrivendo una linea con il piombo.

El llapis està escorcollant una línia amb el plom.

The pencil is scribbling a line with the lead.

Name

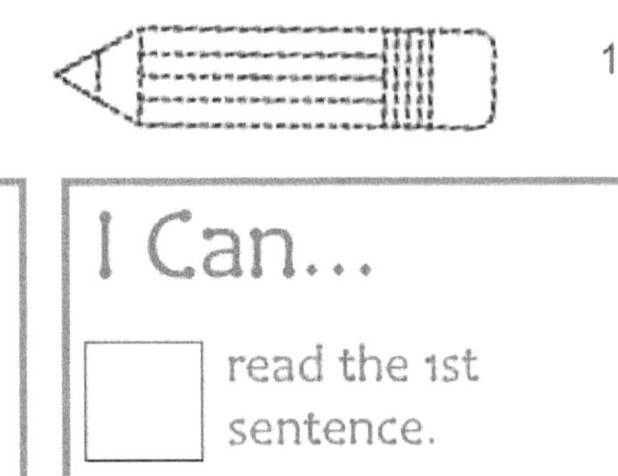

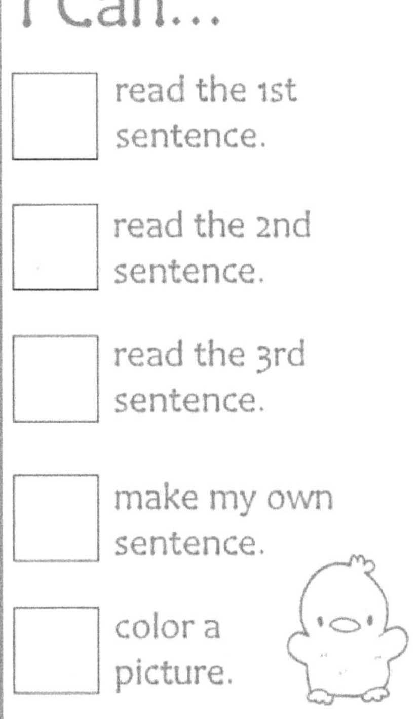

I Can...

- [ ] read the 1st sentence.
- [ ] read the 2nd sentence.
- [ ] read the 3rd sentence.
- [ ] make my own sentence.
- [ ] color a picture.

La matita fece un grande sorriso e andò a lavorare.

El llapis es va posar un gran somriure i va anar a treballar.

The pencil put on a big smile and went to work.

La matita si sveglia brillante e presto per andare al lavoro.

El llapis es desperta brillant i aviat per anar a treballar.

The pencil wakes up bright and early to go to work.

Name

I Can...

- [ ] read the 1st sentence.
- [ ] read the 2nd sentence.
- [ ] read the 3rd sentence.
- [ ] make my own sentence.
- [ ] color a picture.

Questo pupazzo di neve è mio amico ed è un aiutante di Babbo Natale.

Aquest ninot de neu és el meu amic i és un ajudant del Pare Noel.

This snowman is my friend, and he is a helper of Santa.

Il pupazzo di neve sta organizzando una festa di Natale.

El ninot de neu fa una festa de Nadal.

The snowman is having a Christmas party.

Name

I Can...

- [ ] read the 1st sentence.
- [ ] read the 2nd sentence.
- [ ] read the 3rd sentence.
- [ ] make my own sentence.
- [ ] color a picture.

Il polpo lavora come chef e serve cibo.

El pop treballa com a xef i serveix menjar.

The octopus is working as a chef and serving food.

Il polpo cucinava cibo delizioso per i suoi amici.

El pop va cuinar deliciós menjar per als seus amics.

The octopus cooked delicious food for its friends.

Name

I Can...

- ☐ read the 1st sentence.
- ☐ read the 2nd sentence.
- ☐ read the 3rd sentence.
- ☐ make my own sentence.
- ☐ color a picture.

Babbo Natale è felice.

El Pare Noel és feliç.

Santa is happy.

Babbo Natale consegna regali ai bambini.

El Pare Noel lliura regals als nens.

Santa Claus is delivering presents to the children.

Name

I Can...

- [ ] read the 1st sentence.
- [ ] read the 2nd sentence.
- [ ] read the 3rd sentence.
- [ ] make my own sentence.
- [ ] color a picture.

All'orso piace mangiare dolci.

A l'ós li agrada menjar dolços.

The bear likes to eat sweets.

L'orsacchiotto marrone indossa un cappello verde brillante.

L'ós de peluix marró porta un barret de color verd brillant.

The brown teddy bear is wearing a bright green hat.

Name ___________________________ 

I Can...

- ☐ read the 1st sentence.
- ☐ read the 2nd sentence.
- ☐ read the 3rd sentence.
- ☐ make my own sentence.
- ☐ color a picture.

Il libro ha una bacchetta.

El llibre té una vareta.

The book has a wand.

Il ragazzo ha ricevuto un personaggio da mago per il suo compleanno.

El noi va rebre una figura d'acció d'assistent pel seu aniversari.

The boy got a wizard action figure for his birthday.

Name 

I Can...

- [ ] read the 1st sentence.
- [ ] read the 2nd sentence.
- [ ] read the 3rd sentence.
- [ ] make my own sentence.
- [ ] color a picture.

L'orso ha un regalo.

L'ós té un regal.

The bear has a present.

L'orsacchiotto sta aprendo il suo secondo regalo.

El peluix està obrint el seu segon regal.

The teddy bear is opening his second present.

Name 

I Can...

- [ ] read the 1st sentence.
- [ ] read the 2nd sentence.
- [ ] read the 3rd sentence.
- [ ] make my own sentence.
- [ ] color a picture.

Babbo Natale distribuirà regali.

El Pare Noel farà regals.

Santa is going to give out presents.

Babbo Natale porta una borsa di pelle piena di regali.

El Pare Noel porta una bossa de cuir plena de regals.

Santa Claus is carrying a leather bag filled with gifts.

Name

I Can...

- [ ] read the 1st sentence.
- [ ] read the 2nd sentence.
- [ ] read the 3rd sentence.
- [ ] make my own sentence.
- [ ] color a picture.

Ho fatto un pupazzo di neve.

Vaig fer un ninot de neu.

I made a snowman.

Il pupazzo di neve aveva appena finito di pulire il cortile.

El ninot de neu acabava de netejar el pati.

The snowman was just done cleaning the yard.

Name 

I Can...

- [ ] read the 1st sentence.
- [ ] read the 2nd sentence.
- [ ] read the 3rd sentence.
- [ ] make my own sentence.
- [ ] color a picture.

Il pappagallo è colorato.

El lloro és de colors.

The parrot is colorful.

Il pappagallo sta solo imparando a volare nel cielo.

El lloro només està aprenent a volar al cel.

The parrot is just learning how to fly in the sky.

Name _______________________

I Can...

- [ ] read the 1st sentence.
- [ ] read the 2nd sentence.
- [ ] read the 3rd sentence.
- [ ] make my own sentence.
- [ ] color a picture.

Ci sono molti animali

Hi ha molts animals.

There are a lot of animals.

Gli animali stanno avendo un pigiama party gigante.

Els animals estan passant un gir dormidor gegant.

The animals are having a giant sleepover.

Name _______________

I Can...

- ☐ read the 1st sentence.
- ☐ read the 2nd sentence.
- ☐ read the 3rd sentence.
- ☐ make my own sentence.
- ☐ color a picture.

L'uomo indossa una cintura.

L'home porta un cinturó.

The man is wearing a belt.

L'uomo verrà a riparare la nave.

L'home ve a arreglar el vaixell.

The man is coming to fix the ship.

Name

I Can...

- [ ] read the 1st sentence.
- [ ] read the 2nd sentence.
- [ ] read the 3rd sentence.
- [ ] make my own sentence.
- [ ] color a picture.

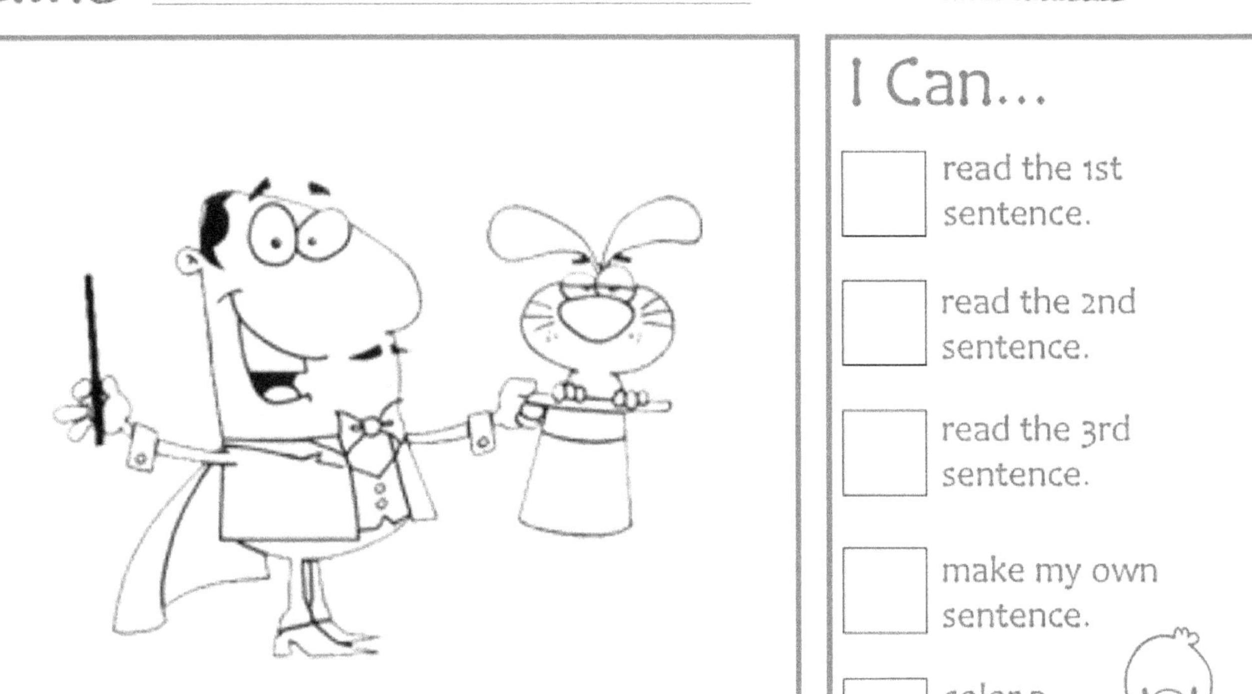

Il coniglio è molto giovane

El conill és molt jove.

The rabbit is very young.

Il mago evocò un coniglio dal suo cappello.

El mag va convocar un conill del barret.

The magician summoned a rabbit out of his hat.

Name ______________________ 

I Can...

- [ ] read the 1st sentence.
- [ ] read the 2nd sentence.
- [ ] read the 3rd sentence.
- [ ] make my own sentence.
- [ ] color a picture.

Ha una pozione.

Ié una roció.

He has a potion.

La donna sta imparando a diventare una scienziata.

La dona està aprenent a convertir-se en científica.

The woman is learning how to become a scientist.

Name _______________________ 

I Can...

- [ ] read the 1st sentence.
- [ ] read the 2nd sentence.
- [ ] read the 3rd sentence.
- [ ] make my own sentence.
- [ ] color a picture.

Indossa occhiali da sole.

Porta ulleres de sol.

He is wearing sunglasses.

Il poliziotto è arrabbiato con alcuni adolescenti marci.

El policia està enfadat amb alguns adolescents podrits.

The policeman is angry at some rotten teenagers.

Name

I Can...

- [ ] read the 1st sentence.
- [ ] read the 2nd sentence.
- [ ] read the 3rd sentence.
- [ ] make my own sentence.
- [ ] color a picture.

Ha un secchio di vernice.

Ié una galleda de pintura.

He has a bucket of paint.

Il pittore di casa ha quasi finito con il suo lavoro quotidiano.

El pintor de casa està gairebé acabat amb la seva feina diària.

The house painter is almost done with his daily work.

Name

I Can...

- [ ] read the 1st sentence.
- [ ] read the 2nd sentence.
- [ ] read the 3rd sentence.
- [ ] make my own sentence.
- [ ] color a picture.

L'uomo ha un cappello.

L'home té barret.

The man has a hat.

Il postino consegna le poste all'alba.

El carter lliura correus a les altures de l'alba.

The postman is delivering mails at the crack of dawn.

Name

I Can...

- [ ] read the 1st sentence.
- [ ] read the 2nd sentence.
- [ ] read the 3rd sentence.
- [ ] make my own sentence.
- [ ] color a picture.

Ha un walkie-talkie.

I é un walkie talkie.

He has a walkie talkie.

L'uomo d'affari chiama il suo capo.

L'empresari està trucant al seu cap.

The businessman is calling his boss.

Name

I Can...

- [ ] read the 1st sentence.
- [ ] read the 2nd sentence.
- [ ] read the 3rd sentence.
- [ ] make my own sentence.
- [ ] color a picture.

Ha sonno.

Està adormit.

He is sleepy.

L'operaio sta rimorchiando delle scatole pesanti.

El treballador remolca unes caixes pesades.

The workman is towing some heavy boxes.

Name ___________________________ 

I Can...

- ☐ read the 1st sentence.
- ☐ read the 2nd sentence.
- ☐ read the 3rd sentence.
- ☐ make my own sentence.
- ☐ color a picture.

Indossa una cravatta a farfalla.

Porta una corbata.

He is wearing a bowtie.

Il cameriere serve limonata fresca a una famiglia.

El cambrer serveix llimonada fresca a una família.

The waiter is serving fresh lemonade to a family.

Name

I Can...

- [ ] read the 1st sentence.
- [ ] read the 2nd sentence.
- [ ] read the 3rd sentence.
- [ ] make my own sentence.
- [ ] color a picture.

Lui ha una valigia.

Ié una maleta.

He has a suitcase.

L'ingegnere riparerà un'auto blu di fantasia.

L'enginyer arreglarà un cotxe blau de luxe.

The engineer is going to fix a fancy blue car.

Name 

I Can...

- [ ] read the 1st sentence.
- [ ] read the 2nd sentence.
- [ ] read the 3rd sentence.
- [ ] make my own sentence.
- [ ] color a picture.

Lo chef ha un tovagliolo.

El xef té un tovalló.

The chef has a napkin.

Lo chef ha preparato una deliziosa pasta che tutti possono condividere.

El xef va elaborar pasta deliciosa perquè tothom compartís.

The chef made yummy pasta for everyone to share.

Name

I Can...

- [ ] read the 1st sentence.
- [ ] read the 2nd sentence.
- [ ] read the 3rd sentence.
- [ ] make my own sentence.
- [ ] color a picture.

Il gallo ha un grosso becco.

El gall té un bec gros.

The rooster has a big beak.

Il pollo bianco indossa un cappello da artista.

El pollastre blanc porta un barret d'artista.

The white chicken is wearing an artist's hat.

Name

I Can...

- [ ] read the 1st sentence.
- [ ] read the 2nd sentence.
- [ ] read the 3rd sentence.
- [ ] make my own sentence.
- [ ] color a picture.

L'uccello è piccolo.

L'ocell és petit.

The bird is small.

Il piccolo pulcino sta usando il telefono di sua madre per riprodurre musica.

El petit pollet està fent servir el telèfon de la seva mare per reproduir música.

The little chick is using his mother's phone to play music.

Name _______________

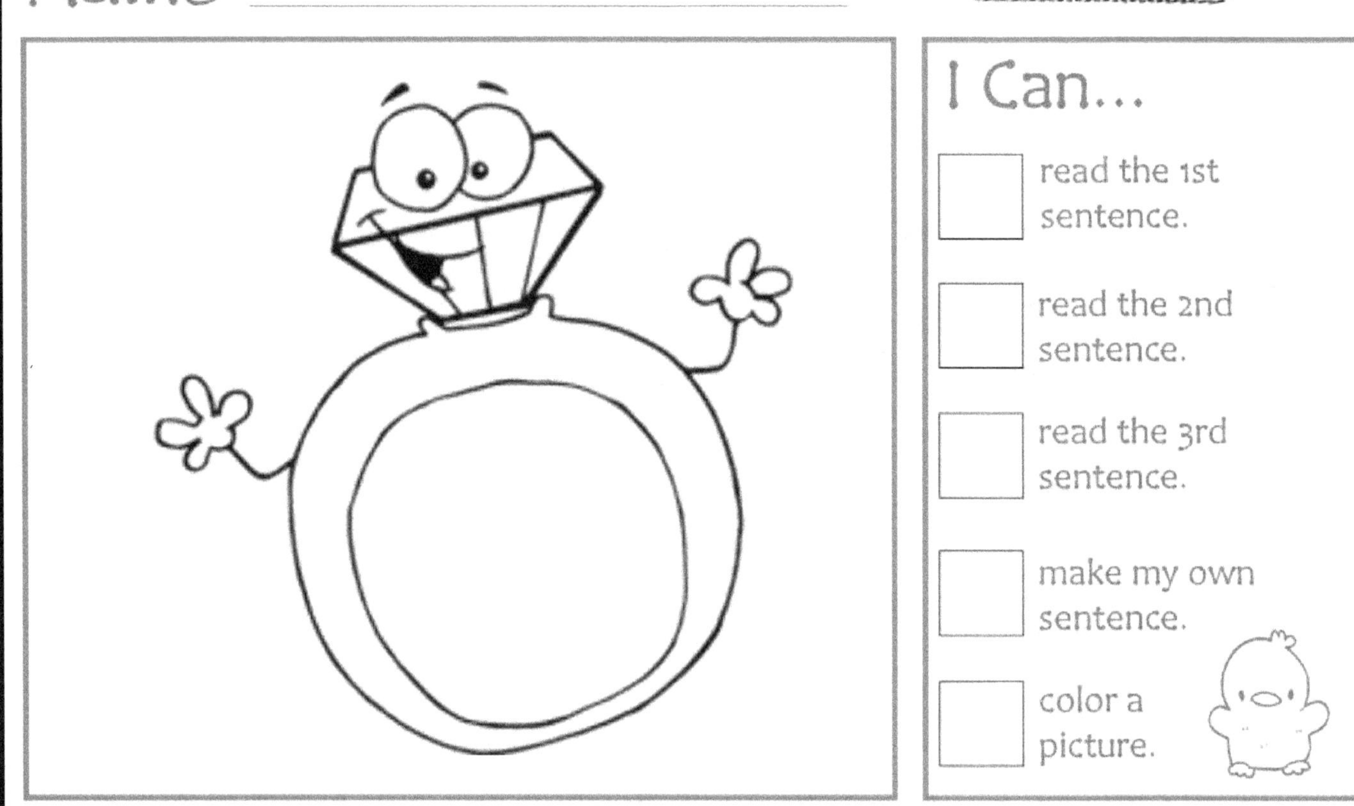

I Can...

- [ ] read the 1st sentence.
- [ ] read the 2nd sentence.
- [ ] read the 3rd sentence.
- [ ] make my own sentence.
- [ ] color a picture.

Questo è il mio anello.

Aquest és el meu anell.

That is my ring.

L'anello ha un gioiello di diamanti.

L'anell té una joia de diamants al damunt.

The ring has a diamond jewel on it.

Name

I Can...

- [ ] read the 1st sentence.
- [ ] read the 2nd sentence.
- [ ] read the 3rd sentence.
- [ ] make my own sentence.
- [ ] color a picture.

L'anatra ha tre uova.

L'ànec té tres ous.

The duck has three eggs.

L'anatra ha appena lasciato cadere le sue piccole uova ovali.

L'ànec acaba de deixar caure els seus petits ous ovalats.

The duck just dropped its little oval eggs.

Name 

I Can...

- [ ] read the 1st sentence.
- [ ] read the 2nd sentence.
- [ ] read the 3rd sentence.
- [ ] make my own sentence.
- [ ] color a picture.

Il cigno è bellissimo.

El cigne és bonic.

The swan is beautiful.

Il bellissimo cigno sta mangiando un pezzo di verdure verdi.

El preciós cigne menja un tros de verdures verdes.

The beautiful swan is eating a piece of green vegetables.

Name ________________

I Can...

- [ ] read the 1st sentence.
- [ ] read the 2nd sentence.
- [ ] read the 3rd sentence.
- [ ] make my own sentence.
- [ ] color a picture.

La ragazza indossa un vestito.

La nena porta un vestit.

The girl is wearing a dress.

La bambina porta due secchi carichi d'acqua.

La petita porta dues galledes molta aigua.

The little girl is carrying two buckets loads of water.

Name _______________ 

I Can...

- [ ] read the 1st sentence.
- [ ] read the 2nd sentence.
- [ ] read the 3rd sentence.
- [ ] make my own sentence.
- [ ] color a picture.

Il ragazzo sta correndo.

El noi corre.

The boy is running.

Il velocista sta conquistando il primo posto in una gara.

El velocista guanya el primer lloc en una cursa.

The sprinter is winning first place in a race.

Name

I Can...

- [ ] read the 1st sentence.
- [ ] read the 2nd sentence.
- [ ] read the 3rd sentence.
- [ ] make my own sentence.
- [ ] color a picture.

Lui è un musicista.

És músic.

He is a musician.

Il ragazzo sta esercitando il flauto per essere pronto a scuola.

El noi està practicant la flauta flauta per estar a punt a l'escola.

The boy is practicing the flute to be ready at school.

Name

I Can...

- [ ] read the 1st sentence.
- [ ] read the 2nd sentence.
- [ ] read the 3rd sentence.
- [ ] make my own sentence.
- [ ] color a picture.

Sembra gioioso.

Es veu alegre.

He looks joyful.

Il batterista sta conducendo una grande parata in costume.

El bateria dirigeix una enorme desfilada de disfresses.

The drummer is leading a huge costume parade.

Name _______________________ 

I Can...

- [ ] read the 1st sentence.
- [ ] read the 2nd sentence.
- [ ] read the 3rd sentence.
- [ ] make my own sentence.
- [ ] color a picture.

Il dinosauro è una rock star.

El dinosaure és una estrella de rock.

The dinosaur is a rock star.

Il sogno del dinosauro è quello di diventare una rockstar meravigliosa.

El somni del dinosaure és convertir-se en una meravellosa estrella de rock.

The dinosaur's dream is to become a wonderful rock star.

Name

L'infermiera aiuta il medico.

La infermera ajuda al metge.

The nurse helps the doctor.

L'infermiera aiuta i pazienti a stare meglio.

La infermera ajuda els pacients a millorar.

The nurse is helping patients get better.

Name

I Can...

- ☐ read the 1st sentence.
- ☐ read the 2nd sentence.
- ☐ read the 3rd sentence.
- ☐ make my own sentence.
- ☐ color a picture.

Indossa una corona.

Porta una corona.

She is wearing a crown.

L'alveare ha un leader che è un'ape magica.

El rusc té un líder que és una abella màgica.

The beehive has a leader who is a magical bee.

Name _______________________________

I Can...

- [ ] read the 1st sentence.
- [ ] read the 2nd sentence.
- [ ] read the 3rd sentence.
- [ ] make my own sentence.
- [ ] color a picture.

È arancione e nero.

És de color taronja i negre.

It is orange and black.

Una tigre formale sta agitando la mano per un taxi giallo.

Un tigre formal està agitant la mà per un taxi groc.

A formal tiger is waving his hand for a yellow taxi.

Name

I Can...

- [ ] read the 1st sentence.
- [ ] read the 2nd sentence.
- [ ] read the 3rd sentence.
- [ ] make my own sentence.
- [ ] color a picture.

Il ragazzo porta molti libri.

El noi porta molts llibres.

The boy is carrying a lot of books.

Il ragazzino intelligente porta libri pesanti da studiare.

El nen intel·ligent porta llibres pesats per estudiar.

The smart little boy is carrying heavy books to study.

Name

I Can...

- [ ] read the 1st sentence.
- [ ] read the 2nd sentence.
- [ ] read the 3rd sentence.
- [ ] make my own sentence.
- [ ] color a picture.

La pizza sembra deliziosa.

La pizza sembla deliciosa.

The pizza looks delicious.

Lo chef ha appena preso il forno per la pizza

El xef acaba de prendre el forn de pizza

The chef just took the pizza oven

Name

I Can...

- [ ] read the 1st sentence.
- [ ] read the 2nd sentence.
- [ ] read the 3rd sentence.
- [ ] make my own sentence.
- [ ] color a picture.

Questo è il computer di mio padre.

Aquest és l'ordinador del meu pare.

That is my dad's computer.

Il laptop sta salutando l'utente.

El portàtil està dient hola a l'usuari.

The laptop is saying hi to the user.

Name

I Can...

- [ ] read the 1st sentence.
- [ ] read the 2nd sentence.
- [ ] read the 3rd sentence.
- [ ] make my own sentence.
- [ ] color a picture.

Il contadino ha la barba.

El pagès té barba.

The farmer has a beard.

Il giardiniere pianterà dei semi.

El jardiner hi plantarà algunes llavors.

The gardener is going to plant some seeds.

Name ___________________________ 

I Can...

- [ ] read the 1st sentence.
- [ ] read the 2nd sentence.
- [ ] read the 3rd sentence.
- [ ] make my own sentence.
- [ ] color a picture.

La fragola è rossa

La maduixa és vermella.

The strawberry is red.

La fragola beve succo freddo rinfrescante.

La maduixa beu suc refrescant fred.

The strawberry is drinking cold refreshing juice.

Name

I Can...

- [ ] read the 1st sentence.
- [ ] read the 2nd sentence.
- [ ] read the 3rd sentence.
- [ ] make my own sentence.
- [ ] color a picture.

Il mago ha una bacchetta.

El mag té una vareta.

The magician has a wand.

Il mago evocherà un grande drago.

L'assistent va a convocar un gran drac.

The wizard is going to summon a great big dragon.

Name _______________________ 

I Can...

- [ ] read the 1st sentence.
- [ ] read the 2nd sentence.
- [ ] read the 3rd sentence.
- [ ] make my own sentence.
- [ ] color a picture.

La renna ha una sciarpa.

Ren té una bufanda.

Reindeer has a scarf.

La renna è in ritardo per dare il suo regalo ai suoi amici.

El ren és tard per donar el present als seus amics.

The reindeer is late to give his present to his friends.

Name

I Can...

- [ ] read the 1st sentence.
- [ ] read the 2nd sentence.
- [ ] read the 3rd sentence.
- [ ] make my own sentence.
- [ ] color a picture.

Ho molte matite.

Tinc molts llapis.

I have a lot of pencils.

Gli utensili per la scrittura sono nel barattolo di latta.

Els estris d'escriptura es troben a la llauna.

The writing utensils are in the tin can.

Name _______________ 

I Can...

- [ ] read the 1st sentence.
- [ ] read the 2nd sentence.
- [ ] read the 3rd sentence.
- [ ] make my own sentence.
- [ ] color a picture.

Babbo Natale è grasso.

El Pare Noel està gros.

Santa is fat.

Babbo Natale sta ridendo di una battuta esilarante.

El Pare Noel es riu d'una broma hilarant.

Santa Claus is laughing at a hilarious joke.

Name

I Can...

- [ ] read the 1st sentence.
- [ ] read the 2nd sentence.
- [ ] read the 3rd sentence.
- [ ] make my own sentence.
- [ ] color a picture.

Ho un naso.

Iinc un nas.

I have one nose.

Il numero uno ha ottenuto il primo posto in una competizione.

El número u va obtenir el primer lloc en una competició.

Number one got first place at a competition.

Name

I Can...

- ☐ read the 1st sentence.
- ☐ read the 2nd sentence.
- ☐ read the 3rd sentence.
- ☐ make my own sentence.
- ☐ color a picture.

Ho due orecchie.

I inc dues orelles.

I have two ears.

Il numero due è in posa per un selfie.

El número dos està present per a un selfie.

Number two is posing for a selfie.

Name ___________________

I Can...

- [ ] read the 1st sentence.
- [ ] read the 2nd sentence.
- [ ] read the 3rd sentence.
- [ ] make my own sentence.
- [ ] color a picture.

Ho tre bottoni sul mio vestito.

Iinc tres botons al meu vestit.

I have three buttons on my dress.

Il numero tre conta fino a tre.

El número tres compta amb tres.

Number three is counting to three.

Name ___________

I Can...

- [ ] read the 1st sentence.
- [ ] read the 2nd sentence.
- [ ] read the 3rd sentence.
- [ ] make my own sentence.
- [ ] color a picture.

Ho 0 code.

I inc 0 cues.

I have 0 tails.

Lo zero dice bene facendo il gesto giusto.

El zero està dient bé fent el gest correcte.

The zero is saying fine by making the okay gesture.

Name _______________ 

I Can...

- [ ] read the 1st sentence.
- [ ] read the 2nd sentence.
- [ ] read the 3rd sentence.
- [ ] make my own sentence.
- [ ] color a picture.

Ho cinque dita su 1 delle mie mani.

linc cinc dits a la meva mà.

I have five fingers on 1 of my hands.

I cinque stanno dicendo il suo nome ad alta voce, quindi altri lo sapranno.

Els cinc diuen el seu nom en veu alta, aixi que altres ho sabran.

Ihe five are saying its name out loud, so others will know.

Name ____________________

I Can...

- [ ] read the 1st sentence.
- [ ] read the 2nd sentence.
- [ ] read the 3rd sentence.
- [ ] make my own sentence.
- [ ] color a picture.

Il mio gatto ha quattro zampe.

El meu gat té quatre potes.

My cat has four legs.

I quattro videro quattro delfini nell'oceano.

Els quatre van veure quatre dofins a l'oceà.

The four saw four dolphins at the ocean.

Name

I Can...

- [ ] read the 1st sentence.
- [ ] read the 2nd sentence.
- [ ] read the 3rd sentence.
- [ ] make my own sentence.
- [ ] color a picture.

Una farfalla ha sei zampe.

Una papallona té sis potes.

A butterfly has six legs.

I sei saltano eccitati su e giù.

Els sis salten emocionats amunt i avall.

The six are excitedly jumping up and down.

Name

I Can...

- [ ] read the 1st sentence.
- [ ] read the 2nd sentence.
- [ ] read the 3rd sentence.
- [ ] make my own sentence.
- [ ] color a picture.

Un ragno ha otto zampe.

Una aranya té vuit potes.

A spider has eight legs.

L'otto si lecca il labbro perché vede otto vassoi di pollo fritto.

El vuit es llepa el llavi perquè veu vuit safates de pollastre fregit.

The eight is licking its lip because it sees eight trays of fried chicken.

Name ____________________ 

I Can...

- [ ] read the 1st sentence.
- [ ] read the 2nd sentence.
- [ ] read the 3rd sentence.
- [ ] make my own sentence.
- [ ] color a picture.

Il gallo sta per svegliare le persone.

El gall va a despertar la gent.

The rooster is going to wake people up.

Il gallo sta svegliando tutti.

El gall està despertant tothom.

The rooster is waking up everybody.

Name

I Can...

- ☐ read the 1st sentence.
- ☐ read the 2nd sentence.
- ☐ read the 3rd sentence.
- ☐ make my own sentence.
- ☐ color a picture.

Mia sorella ha nove animali di peluche.

La meva germana té nou peluixos.

My sister has nine stuffed animals.

Il nove sta dicendo che $4 + 5 = 9$.

El nou diu que $4 + 5 = 9$.

The nine is saying that $4+5=9$.

Name

I Can...

- [ ] read the 1st sentence.
- [ ] read the 2nd sentence.
- [ ] read the 3rd sentence.
- [ ] make my own sentence.
- [ ] color a picture.

L'ape baby ha strisce gialle e nere.

L'abella infantil té ratlles grogues i negres.

The baby bee has yellow and black stripes.

Le api hanno ali molto piccole.

Les abelles bebè tenen les ales molt minúscules.

The baby bees have very tiny wings.

Name ____________________

I Can...

- [ ] read the 1st sentence.
- [ ] read the 2nd sentence.
- [ ] read the 3rd sentence.
- [ ] make my own sentence.
- [ ] color a picture.

La coccinella ha molti punti.

La marieta té molts punts.

The ladybug has many spots.

La coccinella sta mangiando un pezzo di lattuga.

La marieta està menjant un tros d'enciam.

The ladybug is eating a piece of lettuce.

Name

I Can...

- [ ] read the 1st sentence.
- [ ] read the 2nd sentence.
- [ ] read the 3rd sentence.
- [ ] make my own sentence.
- [ ] color a picture.

Le pecore sono magre.

Les ovelles són primes.

The sheep are skinny.

Questa pecora è così soffice.

Aquesta ovella és tan esponjosa.

This sheep is so fluffy.

Name 

I Can...

- [ ] read the 1st sentence.
- [ ] read the 2nd sentence.
- [ ] read the 3rd sentence.
- [ ] make my own sentence.
- [ ] color a picture.

Il coniglio partecipa a una gara di pittura di uova.

El conill participa en un concurs de pintura d'òvuls.

The rabbit is entering an egg painting contest.

Al coniglietto pasquale piace dipingere le uova.

Al conill de Pasqua li agrada pintar ous.

The Easter Bunny likes to paint eggs.

Name

I Can...

- [ ] read the 1st sentence.
- [ ] read the 2nd sentence.
- [ ] read the 3rd sentence.
- [ ] make my own sentence.
- [ ] color a picture.

Il gufo è un insegnante di arti linguistiche.

El mussol és professor d'arts d'idiomes.

The owl is a language arts teacher.

Mr. Owl insegna in terza elementare.

Mr.Owl ensenya el 3r de primària.

Mr.Owl teaches the 3rd grade.

Name

I Can...

- ☐ read the 1st sentence.
- ☐ read the 2nd sentence.
- ☐ read the 3rd sentence.
- ☐ make my own sentence.
- ☐ color a picture.

L'uomo ha un martello antico.

L'home té un martell antic.

The man has an ancient hammer.

L'uomo ha comprato un nuovo martello lucido.

L'home ha comprat un martell nou i brillant.

The man has bought a shiny new hammer.

Name

I Can...

- [ ] read the 1st sentence.
- [ ] read the 2nd sentence.
- [ ] read the 3rd sentence.
- [ ] make my own sentence.
- [ ] color a picture.

La capra ha un amico.

La cabra té un amic.

The goat has a friend.

La capra ha quattro zoccoli.

La cabra té quatre peülles.

The goat has four hooves.

Name

I Can...

- [ ] read the 1st sentence.
- [ ] read the 2nd sentence.
- [ ] read the 3rd sentence.
- [ ] make my own sentence.
- [ ] color a picture.

L'amica di mia mamma è una domestica.

L'amiga de la meva mare és donzella.

My mom's friend is a maid.

La cameriera ha una grande scopa marrone.

La criada té una gran escombra marró.

The maid has a big brown broom.

Name ___________

I Can...

- [ ] read the 1st sentence.
- [ ] read the 2nd sentence.
- [ ] read the 3rd sentence.
- [ ] make my own sentence.
- [ ] color a picture.

Sono andato allo zoo.

Vaig anar al zoo.

I went to the zoo.

Gli animali hanno invitato la scimmia e il pappagallo a unirsi al loro pigiama party.

Els animals van convidar el mico i el lloro a unir-se a la seva festa de dormir.

The animals invited the monkey and the parrot to join their sleepover.

Name

I Can...

- [ ] read the 1st sentence.
- [ ] read the 2nd sentence.
- [ ] read the 3rd sentence.
- [ ] make my own sentence.
- [ ] color a picture.

Il dinosauro ha un cuscino.

El dinosaure té un coixí.

The dinosaur has a pillow.

Il dinosauro sta ottenendo un piatto per il suo cibo.

El dinosaure està aconseguint un plat per menjar.

The dinosaur is getting a plate for his food.

Name

I Can...

- [ ] read the 1st sentence.
- [ ] read the 2nd sentence.
- [ ] read the 3rd sentence.
- [ ] make my own sentence.
- [ ] color a picture.

Il ragazzo è entusiasta di andare a scuola.

El noi està emocionat per anar a l'escola.

The boy is excited to go to school.

Il ragazzo si sta preparando per la scuola.

El noi es prepara per a l'escola.

The boy is preparing for school.

Name

I Can...

- [ ] read the 1st sentence.
- [ ] read the 2nd sentence.
- [ ] read the 3rd sentence.
- [ ] make my own sentence.
- [ ] color a picture.

I bambini sullo scuolabus vanno a scuola.

Els nens de l'autobús escolar van a l'escola.

The kids on the school bus are going to school.

I bambini vanno a scuola su un autobus.

Els nens van a l'escola en un autobús.

The children go to school on a bus.

Name

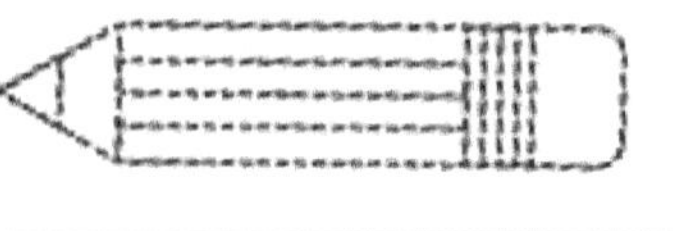

I Can...

- [ ] read the 1st sentence.
- [ ] read the 2nd sentence.
- [ ] read the 3rd sentence.
- [ ] make my own sentence.
- [ ] color a picture.

Il cobra è adorabile.

La cobra és molt maca.

The cobra is very lovely.

L'anaconda è il serpente più lungo del mondo.

L'anaconda és la serp més llarga del món.

The anaconda is the longest snake in the world.

Name

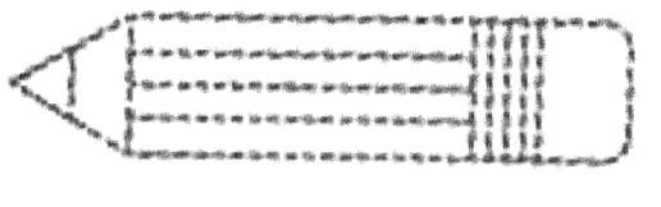

I Can...

- [ ] read the 1st sentence.
- [ ] read the 2nd sentence.
- [ ] read the 3rd sentence.
- [ ] make my own sentence.
- [ ] color a picture.

Questo è un cane grasso!

Això és un gos gros

That is a fat dog!

Il cane ha un colletto d'oro.

El gos té un collet daurat.

The dog has a golden collar.

Name _______________________

I Can...

- [ ] read the 1st sentence.
- [ ] read the 2nd sentence.
- [ ] read the 3rd sentence.
- [ ] make my own sentence.
- [ ] color a picture.

L'elefante vive nello zoo.

L'elefant viu al zoo.

The elephant lives in the zoo.

L'elefante ha un tronco lungo.

L'elefant té un tronc llarg.

The elephant has a long trunk.

Name

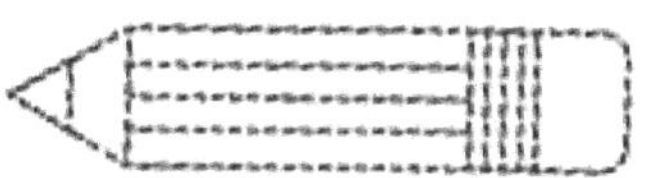

I Can...

- [ ] read the 1st sentence.
- [ ] read the 2nd sentence.
- [ ] read the 3rd sentence.
- [ ] make my own sentence.
- [ ] color a picture.

La giraffa mangia verdure.

La girafa menja verdures.

The giraffe eats vegetables.

La giraffa ha molti punti.

La girafa té molts punts.

The giraffe has many spots.

Name

I Can...

- [ ] read the 1st sentence.
- [ ] read the 2nd sentence.
- [ ] read the 3rd sentence.
- [ ] make my own sentence.
- [ ] color a picture.

Lo scoiattolo ha una pancia morbida.

El xip té una panxa suau.

The chipmunk has a soft tummy.

La tamia ha portato a casa una ghianda gigante.

El xip va portar a casa una gla gegant.

The chipmunk brought home a giant acorn.

I Can...

- ☐ read the 1st sentence.
- ☐ read the 2nd sentence.
- ☐ read the 3rd sentence.
- ☐ make my own sentence.
- ☐ color a picture.

Ho dieci dita in totale.

I inc deu dits de punta en total.

I have ten toes in total.

Uno e Zero insieme sono dieci.

Un i zero són deu.

One and Zero together are ten.

Name

I Can...

- [ ] read the 1st sentence.
- [ ] read the 2nd sentence.
- [ ] read the 3rd sentence.
- [ ] make my own sentence.
- [ ] color a picture.

L'alligatore sta saltando.

L'aligator està saltant.

The alligator is jumping.

Il coccodrillo che salta è felice.

El cocodril saltant és feliç.

The jumping crocodile is happy.

Name 

I Can...

- [ ] read the 1st sentence.
- [ ] read the 2nd sentence.
- [ ] read the 3rd sentence.
- [ ] make my own sentence.
- [ ] color a picture.

Ho trovato una formica.

Vaig trobar una formiga.

I found an ant.

Una formica è di taglia piccola, ma molto forte.

Una formiga té una mida petita, però molt forta.

An ant is tiny in size, but very strong.

Name

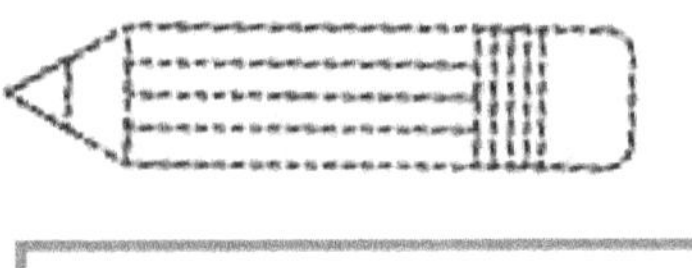

I Can...

- [ ] read the 1st sentence.
- [ ] read the 2nd sentence.
- [ ] read the 3rd sentence.
- [ ] make my own sentence.
- [ ] color a picture.

Il pipistrello dorme a testa in giù.

El ratpenat dorm al revés.

The bat sleeps upside down.

Il pipistrello abbraccia la lettera.

El ratpenat està abraçant la carta.

The bat is hugging the letter.

Name

I Can...

- ☐ read the 1st sentence.
- ☐ read the 2nd sentence.
- ☐ read the 3rd sentence.
- ☐ make my own sentence.
- ☐ color a picture.

Il gatto è molto stanco.

El gat està molt cansat.

The cat is very tired.

Il gatto ha molto sonno.

El gat està molt adormit.

The cat is very sleepy.

Name

I Can...

- [ ] read the 1st sentence.
- [ ] read the 2nd sentence.
- [ ] read the 3rd sentence.
- [ ] make my own sentence.
- [ ] color a picture.

Al cane piace giocare.

Al gos li agrada jugar.

The dog likes to play.

Al cane piace leccare l'osso.

Al gos li agrada llepar-se l'os.

The dog likes to lick the bone.

Name

I Can...

- ☐ read the 1st sentence.
- ☐ read the 2nd sentence.
- ☐ read the 3rd sentence.
- ☐ make my own sentence.
- ☐ color a picture.

L'elefante ha le ciglia.

L'elefant té pestanyes.

The elephant has eyelashes.

L'elefante ha orecchie grandi.

L'elefant té grans orelles.

The elephant has big ears.

Name _______________________ 

I Can...

- [ ] read the 1st sentence.
- [ ] read the 2nd sentence.
- [ ] read the 3rd sentence.
- [ ] make my own sentence.
- [ ] color a picture.

La rana sta saltellando.

La granota està saltant.

The frog is hopping.

La rana usa la lingua per catturare la preda.

La granota utilitza la llengua per atrapar preses.

The frog uses its tongue to catch prey.

Name

I Can...

- [ ] read the 1st sentence.
- [ ] read the 2nd sentence.
- [ ] read the 3rd sentence.
- [ ] make my own sentence.
- [ ] color a picture.

La capra cammina assonnata.

La cabra està caminant per dormir.

The goat is sleepily walking around.

La capra sta pascendo nel prato.

La cabra està pasturant al prat.

The goat is grazing in the meadow.

Name

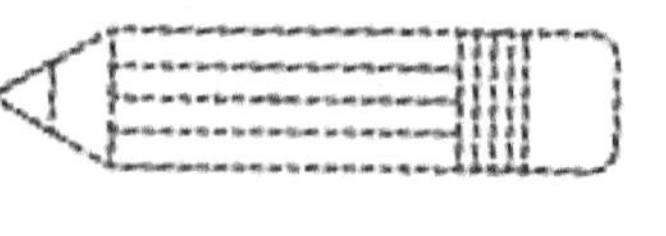

I Can...

- ☐ read the 1st sentence.
- ☐ read the 2nd sentence.
- ☐ read the 3rd sentence.
- ☐ make my own sentence.
- ☐ color a picture.

L'ippopotamo ha una testa grande.

L'hipopòtam té un cap gros.

The hippo has a big head.

L'ippopotamo è stupito di quanto siano grandi i suoi denti.

L'hipopòtam queda sorprès de com de grans són les dents.

The hippo is amazed at how big his teeth are.

Name _______________________

I Can...

- [ ] read the 1st sentence.
- [ ] read the 2nd sentence.
- [ ] read the 3rd sentence.
- [ ] make my own sentence.
- [ ] color a picture.

L'iguana ha una coda lunga.

L'iguana té una cua llarga.

The iguana has a long tail.

L'iguana si sta avvolgendo attorno all'alfabeto.

L'iguana s'enrotlla a l'alfabet.

The iguana is curling around the alphabet.

Name

I Can...

- [ ] read the 1st sentence.
- [ ] read the 2nd sentence.
- [ ] read the 3rd sentence.
- [ ] make my own sentence.
- [ ] color a picture.

La mamma ha comprato una nuova bottiglia di marmellata.

La mare va comprar una nova ampolla de melmelada.

Mom bought a new bottle of jam.

Puoi mettere la marmellata sul toast per dargli più gusto.

Podeu posar melmelada a la torrada per donar-li més gust.

You can put jam on toast to give it more taste.

Name

I Can...

- [ ] read the 1st sentence.
- [ ] read the 2nd sentence.
- [ ] read the 3rd sentence.
- [ ] make my own sentence.
- [ ] color a picture.

L'aquilone ha una bellissima coda.

El estel té una bonica cua.

The kite has a beautiful tail.

L'aquilone è a terra.

El estel està a terra.

The kite is on the ground.

Name ____________________

I Can...

- [ ] read the 1st sentence.
- [ ] read the 2nd sentence.
- [ ] read the 3rd sentence.
- [ ] make my own sentence.
- [ ] color a picture.

Il leone è timido.

El lleó és tímid.

The lion is timid.

Il leone sta inseguendo la coda.

El lleó està perseguint la cua.

The lion is chasing its tail.

Name

I Can...

- [ ] read the 1st sentence.
- [ ] read the 2nd sentence.
- [ ] read the 3rd sentence.
- [ ] make my own sentence.
- [ ] color a picture.

Mi piacciono i topi.

M'agraden els ratolins.

I like mice.

Il mouse ha baffi molto lunghi.

El ratolí té bigotis molt llargs.

The mouse has very long whiskers.

Name ____________________

I Can...

- ☐ read the 1st sentence.
- ☐ read the 2nd sentence.
- ☐ read the 3rd sentence.
- ☐ make my own sentence.
- ☐ color a picture.

Il naso sta respirando.

El nas respira.

The nose is breathing.

Il naso è usato per annusare le cose.

El nas s'utilitza per olorar coses.

The nose is used for smelling things.

Name

I Can...

- [ ] read the 1st sentence.
- [ ] read the 2nd sentence.
- [ ] read the 3rd sentence.
- [ ] make my own sentence.
- [ ] color a picture.

Il polpo vive sott'acqua.

El pulp viu sota l'aigua.

The octopus lives underwater.

Il polpo ha tentacoli molto lunghi.

El pop té tentacles molt llargs.

The octopus has very long tentacles.

Name

I Can...

- [ ] read the 1st sentence.
- [ ] read the 2nd sentence.
- [ ] read the 3rd sentence.
- [ ] make my own sentence.
- [ ] color a picture.

Il pinguino mangia pesce.

El pingüí menja peixos.

The penguin eats fish.

Il pinguino vive nelle regioni fredde.

El pingüí viu a les regions fredes.

The penguin lives in cold regions.

Name _______________

I Can...

- [ ] read the 1st sentence.
- [ ] read the 2nd sentence.
- [ ] read the 3rd sentence.
- [ ] make my own sentence.
- [ ] color a picture.

La regina ha una bacchetta.

La reina té una vareta.

The queen has a wand.

La regina ha una bacchetta rosa.

La reina té una vareta rosa.

The queen has a pink wand.

Name ___________

I Can...

- [ ] read the 1st sentence.
- [ ] read the 2nd sentence.
- [ ] read the 3rd sentence.
- [ ] make my own sentence.
- [ ] color a picture.

Il coniglio ha le orecchie lunghe.

El conill té unes orelles llargues.

The rabbit has long ears.

Il coniglio è confuso.

El conill es confon.

The rabbit is confused.

Name

I Can...

- [ ] read the 1st sentence.
- [ ] read the 2nd sentence.
- [ ] read the 3rd sentence.
- [ ] make my own sentence.
- [ ] color a picture.

Il serpente ha pois.

La serp té polques.

The snake has polka dots.

Il serpente è molto viscido.

La serp és molt prim.

The snake is very slimy.

Name

I Can...

- [ ] read the 1st sentence.
- [ ] read the 2nd sentence.
- [ ] read the 3rd sentence.
- [ ] make my own sentence.
- [ ] color a picture.

La tartaruga ha un guscio appuntito.

La tortuga té una closca punxeguda.

The tortoise has a pointy shell.

La tartaruga vive sulla terra, a differenza delle tartarughe.

La tortuga viu a la terra, a diferència de les tortugues.

The tortoise lives on land, unlike turtles.

Name

I Can...

- [ ] read the 1st sentence.
- [ ] read the 2nd sentence.
- [ ] read the 3rd sentence.
- [ ] make my own sentence.
- [ ] color a picture.

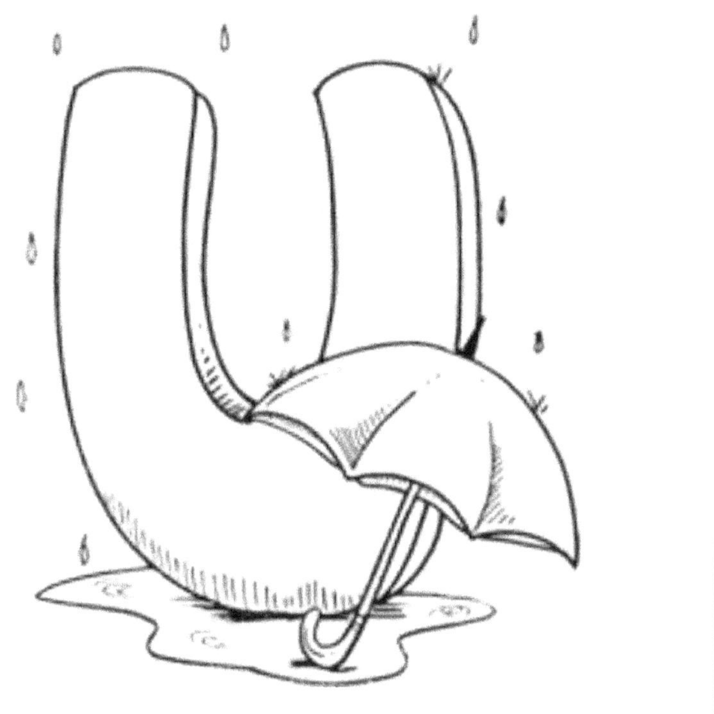

Piove.

Està plovent.

It's raining.

L'ombrello ti protegge.

El paraigua et resguarda.

The umbrella shelters you.

Name

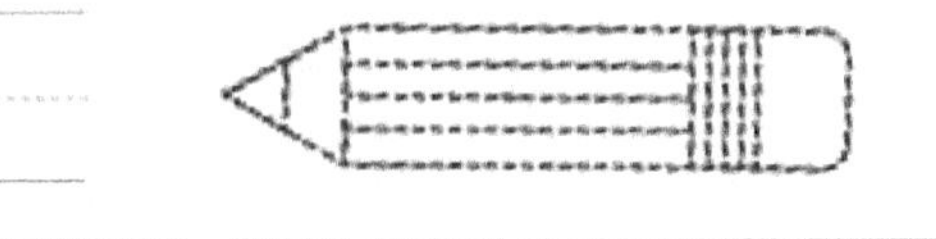

I Can...

- [ ] read the 1st sentence.
- [ ] read the 2nd sentence.
- [ ] read the 3rd sentence.
- [ ] make my own sentence.
- [ ] color a picture.

Il violino è uno strumento musicale.

El violí és un instrument musical.

The violin is a musical instrument.

Il violino è uno degli strumenti più fantastici.

El violí és un dels instruments més fantàstics.

The violin is one of the most fantastic instruments.

Name

I Can...

- [ ] read the 1st sentence.
- [ ] read the 2nd sentence.
- [ ] read the 3rd sentence.
- [ ] make my own sentence.
- [ ] color a picture.

Il tricheco ha un amico.

La morsa té un amic.

The walrus has a friend.

Il tricheco ha una coda.

La morsa té cua.

The walrus has a tail.

Name

I Can...

- [ ] read the 1st sentence.
- [ ] read the 2nd sentence.
- [ ] read the 3rd sentence.
- [ ] make my own sentence.
- [ ] color a picture.

Lo xilofono è uno strumento colorato.

El xilòfon és un instrument de colors.

The xylophone is a colorful instrument.

Lo xilofono è uno strumento molto interessante.

El xilòfon és un instrument molt maco.

The xylophone is a very cool instrument.

Name

I Can...

- [ ] read the 1st sentence.
- [ ] read the 2nd sentence.
- [ ] read the 3rd sentence.
- [ ] make my own sentence.
- [ ] color a picture.

Il ragazzo ha un cappellino.

El noi té una mica de barret.

The boy has a little hat.

Il bambino ha uno yoyo molto colorato.

El noi té un yoyo molt vistós.

The kid has a very colorful yoyo.

Name

I Can...

- [ ] read the 1st sentence.
- [ ] read the 2nd sentence.
- [ ] read the 3rd sentence.
- [ ] make my own sentence.
- [ ] color a picture.

La zebra ha una coda.

La zebra té cua.

The zebra has a tail.

La zebra sorride ampiamente

La zebra somriu àmpliament

The zebra is smiling widely

Name 

I Can...

- [ ] read the 1st sentence.
- [ ] read the 2nd sentence.
- [ ] read the 3rd sentence.
- [ ] make my own sentence.
- [ ] color a picture.

Ho una candela sulla mia torta.

Iinc una espelma al meu pastís.

I have a candle on my cake.

Questa torta di compleanno è per un bambino.

Aquest pastís d'aniversari és per a un nen petit.

This birthday cake is for a little kids.

Name

I Can...

- [ ] read the 1st sentence.
- [ ] read the 2nd sentence.
- [ ] read the 3rd sentence.
- [ ] make my own sentence.
- [ ] color a picture.

L'astronauta sta andando in missione.

L'astronauta segueix una missió.

The astronaut is going on a mission.

L'astronauta vide qualcosa in lontananza.

L'astronauta va veure alguna cosa a la distància.

The astronaut saw something in the distance.

Name

I Can...

- [ ] read the 1st sentence.
- [ ] read the 2nd sentence.
- [ ] read the 3rd sentence.
- [ ] make my own sentence.
- [ ] color a picture.

Il samurai sta andando a fare jogging mattutino.

El samurai va a buscar un matí.

The samurai is going for a morning jog.

Il samurai sta inseguendo il suo nemico.

El samurai persegueix al seu enemic.

The samurai is chasing away his enemy.

Name

I Can...

- [ ] read the 1st sentence.
- [ ] read the 2nd sentence.
- [ ] read the 3rd sentence.
- [ ] make my own sentence.
- [ ] color a picture.

Il mio amico sta mangiando una torta gigantesca.

El meu amic està tenint un pastís gegantesc.

My friend is having a gigantic cake.

Questa torta di compleanno ha tre strati.

Aquest pastís d'aniversari té tres capes.

This birthday cake has three layers.

Name ____________________

I Can...

- ☐ read the 1st sentence.
- ☐ read the 2nd sentence.
- ☐ read the 3rd sentence.
- ☐ make my own sentence.
- ☐ color a picture.

La rana sta inseguendo la mosca.

La granota persegueix la mosca.

The frog is chasing the fly.

La rana sta prendendo una mosca.

La granota està agafant una mosca.

The frog is catching a fly.

www.ingramcontent.com/pod-product-compliance
Lightning Source LLC
Chambersburg PA
CBHW081345160726
48000CB00010B/3237